# Lessons from the

# Western Warriors

## Dynamic Self-Defense Techniques

# Lessons from the

# Western Warriors

## Dynamic Self-Defense Techniques

## Fred Neff
### Photographs by Bob Wolfe

## Lerner Publications Company • Minneapolis

The models photographed in this book are Richard DeValerio, John H. Wong, Michelle Wong, Michael C. Wong, Christa Powell, Andre Louis Richardson, James Louis Blakey, Jim Reid, Robert Wolfe, and Douglas R. Shrewsbury.

LIBRARY OF CONGRESS CATALOGING-IN-PUBLICATION DATA

**Neff, Fred.**
    Lessons from the western warriors.

    (Fred Neff's secrets of self-defense)
    Includes index.
    Summary: Examines methods of hand-to-hand fighting developed from the Greeks and other Western peoples, contrasts them with the Eastern martial arts, and gives instructions in using boxing and other techniques in self-defense.
    1. Self-defense—Juvenile literature. 2. Hand-to-hand fighting—History—Juvenile literature. 3. Wrestling—Juvenile literature. 4. Boxing—Juvenile literature. [1. Self-defense. 2. Hand-to-hand fighting. 3. Boxing] I. Wolfe, Robert L., ill. II. Title. III. Series: Neff, Fred. Fred Neff's secrets of self-defense.
GV1111.N453    1987                  613.6'6                  86-21151
ISBN 0-8225-1159-2 (lib. bdg.)

Manufactured in the United States of America

International Standard Book Number: 0-8225-1159-2
Library of Congress Catalog Card Number: 86-21151

2   3   4   5   6   7   8   9   10   97   96   95   94   93   92   91   90   89   88

*To Major Barney Neff, fighter pilot, master of self-defense, and humanitarian, whose unselfish kindness and devotion to helping other people made the world a little bit better place.*

# CONTENTS

When I was a small boy, my uncle Major Barney Neff introduced me to the wonders of the fighting arts. He took me regularly to the gym, and I watched as he taught the intricacies of self-defense. The most mundane fighting techniques were graceful and effective as he taught them. All who learned from him were truly fortunate. Equally important, he set an example of quiet confidence, not bragging or showing off his skill in his private life. He demonstrated the knowledge, strength, skill, and concern for others of a true master of self-defense. I have been impressed with Western self-protection methods ever since.

Traditionally, students of Eastern martial arts and of Western sports such as boxing and wrestling have scorned each other's techniques. I have been asked many times to compare Western fighting techniques with Eastern martial arts in power and effectiveness. This book answers some of these common questions and explains Western fighting techniques.

The techniques that follow are not for sport, but are examples of Western hitting and grappling methods that can be combined carefully to defend oneself. This book is not meant to be a boxing or wrestling primer. It should, however, teach readers how to use Western self-defense methods better.

I hope that this book will give Eastern martial arts enthusiasts greater respect and understanding for Western fighting forms. Western fighters and Eastern martial arts practitioners have a common interest in self-defense. They will benefit physically, mentally, and emotionally, from respecting one another and opening their minds to others' thoughts and methods.

*Greek grappling, the ancestor of modern wrestling.*

# INTRODUCTION

The last decade has brought a tremendous interest in karate, kempo, kung fu, and other arts from the East. Are there no Western self-defense methods to be studied? The answer is that Western fighting techniques are camouflaged as the sports of wrestling and boxing.

Culture plays a large part in developing fighting forms. In ancient times, people in Eastern countries often faced life-and-death struggles, yet only a small number of elite were allowed to possess weapons. The common people needed to develop methods of unarmed combat. In the West, weapons were usually available and there were laws against certain types of violence, so unarmed self-defense systems were not needed.

The most ancient form of self-defense was probably wrestling. Two children in a playground fight still show the natural tendency to grab and wrestle. Early mankind often supplemented grappling techniques with wide, swinging punches, now known as *hooks*. Later, soldiers often fought with weapons, such as clubs or spears, which gave them more power and reach. Grappling and punching were used

only when fighters were disarmed or too close to each other for weapons to be effective. As weapons became more effective, soldiers had less need for personal self-defense techniques in war. Punching or hitting techniques and wrestling were kept active in the West primarily as games or sports.

Among the first Western peoples to organize wrestling techniques into a sport were the ancient Hebrews. Scenes of what look to be boxing and wrestling contests have also been found in ruins of ancient Babylon. The ancient Egyptians also appear to have practiced a form of wrestling.

The clearest picture we have of the development of sports from combat methods comes from the Greeks. The Greeks created the sports of boxing, wrestling, and *pankration*. Their boxing matches were very violent, crude affairs. The boxer primarily blocked with his forward arm and threw punches with the other. The crude, hooking and clubbing punches were powerful—but inefficient. Greek wrestling, however, was highly developed. The sport was based on practical lessons learned in warfare. The Greeks also developed pankration, which may have been the first complete Western self-defense system. So popular was pankration that it is believed to have been a part of ancient Olympic Games. The goal of the sport was to force an opponent to give up. Nearly any unarmed technique was allowed—punching, kicking, throwing, choking, and joint locks included. The great conqueror Alexander the Great was known to be an admirer of this brutal art and probably spread its use wherever his troops traveled. No doubt Greeks trained in pankration were effective in hand-to-hand fighting. It may have been a significant factor in Alexander's success. It is possible that Greek fighting techniques influenced the fighting methods in Eastern countries exposed to them. The art of pankration died out in Greece as people became more interested in safety in sports.

The Romans learned many fighting methods from the Greeks. However, they used a spiked and weighted glove in certain fist-fighting matches. The fighters learned to place less emphasis on boxing methods and more on the glove as a weapon. As a result, interest in boxing appears to have declined. Interest increased in wrestling and weaponry techniques as sports and in combat. Romans spread their fighting methods throughout Europe to the lands they conquered.

Medieval Europeans had little interest in boxing and considered wrestling a better sport. Most people enjoyed watching wrestling, and in matches soldiers could learn elementary holds and throws used in close combat. Sword fighting, however, was considered by many medieval people to be the primary sport and method of self-defense.

Out of medieval Europe came a special class of people known as knights. They were trained in riding, weaponry, and wrestling. The nobility preferred weaponry to hand-to-hand combat in public contests. Ordinary people were the real developers of wrestling in this period. Later, in fifteenth century England, skilled warriors called *masters of the noble arts of self-defense* set up classes in the techniques of fighting with staff and sword, and in related hand-to-hand combat.

As time went on, the English started to use movements in boxing similar to those used in fencing. In eighteenth century England, James Figg, a great master of fighting, brought together techniques from wrestling, boxing, and fencing. He opened a school of self-defense and was recognized by many as a boxing champion. The sport was very crude and brutal in Figg's day. Bare-knuckle fighting and wrestling throws were still allowed. The punches were often either hooks or crude movements in which the attacker jumped as he punched to gain power. The goal of a match was not just to knock out the opponent but to control the situation as one would in a real fight. The English spread their knowledge of and enthusiasm for boxing throughout Europe.

In early eighteenth century France, a new art of foot-fighting, commonly known as *savate*, had begun. Over time

*Early nineteenth century fisticuffs, the foundation for modern boxing.*

it became a popular sport. It combined kicking techniques with some hand techniques. The English influenced French kicking experts to add more boxing-type hand techniques to their art. As years went by, kicking techniques gradually worked into defense methods throughout the world.

By the middle of the nineteenth century, wrestling and boxing were very popular sports in Europe. Wrestlers began to favor leverage and scientific methods over striking techniques. Boxing also became more polished when the use of throws was discouraged and more effective punches were developed.

Although boxers had occasionally used a straight punch, it was not until near the end of the nineteenth century

that James J. Corbett made this punch popular. Scientific boxing strategy took a large step forward with Corbett's use of the straight punch and of effective movement. He taught by example that a straight punch can not only be faster than a hook, but also of much greater accuracy. This punch was a great advance over the crude, clubbing type of punches common at the time.

By the 1920s, boxing had developed into a modern art that had strategy, grace, and efficient method. Wrestling also became more standardized, streamlined, and efficient. Participants had a strong knowledge of anatomy, leverage, throws, and holds.

Today, many people have been exposed to amateur wrestling and boxing. However, the public often overlooks the fact that each of these sports contains fighting techniques that are efficient, powerful, and relatively easy to learn. Military agencies have trained their personnel in techniques from these sports. Anyone who is in good health and willing to work on skills can learn these techniques.

This book will introduce certain Western self-defense methods from the modern sports of boxing and wrestling, along with some kicking methods. The techniques outlined here may differ slightly from the sporting application because of the practical needs of self-protection. An attacker in a street brawl won't play by the rules.

I hope this book will answer many questions asked by martial arts enthusiasts about the practical applications of Western fighting techniques.

# COMMON QUESTIONS

### 1. Are Western fighting techniques practical for self-defense?

Western self-protection techniques have proven over time to be effective in defending against a single, unarmed attacker. It is true that when you use only boxing or wrestling techniques, you may lose some of the effectiveness of the system. This is because distance plays a large part in determining whether boxing or wrestling techniques are most useful. However, the individual who is trained in both boxing and wrestling has a well-rounded set of defenses.

### 2. Will Western self-protection techniques allow a small person to overcome a powerful bully?

Yes. Western self-defense methods can help a small person to protect himself or herself against a strong aggressor. Western self-defense methods include specific strategies for persons of different body types so everyone can obtain maximum effectiveness. Both Western and Eastern self-defense methods are based on the belief that presence of mind, self-confidence, speed, timing, and persistence can make a difference in the outcome of a fight. It is not necessarily the sizes of the fighters or their relative strengths that determine who wins.

### 3. Is there a way to handle a bully so I do not have to fight?

Sometimes it is very difficult for a person to get out of a confrontation. Bullies tend to focus on people they believe are frightened of them. Develop the attitude that verbal abuse or bad conduct has to be expected of others. Do not lose your temper just because someone is obnoxious. Walk away and avoid people that upset you. If you are in a situation from which you cannot easily walk away, then look the attacker confidently in the eye and exhibit no fear. Often simply showing confidence and walking away will end any abuse. You must also not court attack by your attitude or by bragging. No one earns respect by telling people "I am tough." Bold statements encourage confrontations. The best fighters are those confident enough not to brag.

### 4. Are there any basic principles that will help me to win a confrontation?

These five general principles of self-protection will help in any confrontation:

1. Keep calm. When you're calm, you can think and act quickly, and speed is a key consideration in any fight. Even a relatively unskilled fighter can win out over a powerful aggressor, if he or she keeps cool. If you keep your mind on your strategy, you will remain calmer than if you worry about what harm may come to you. A calm manner will impress the attacker that you have self-confidence and are not afraid. This alone may end the fight.

2. Exploit weak points. Every human body has sensitive spots. When facing an aggressor, try to plan an attack on one of these spots. Some of the most sensitive areas of the body are the shins, knees, groin, stomach, ribs, solar plexus, chin, jaw, face, and temple (*see diagram*). If you can quickly hit one of these spots you will take some of the fight out of the aggressor.

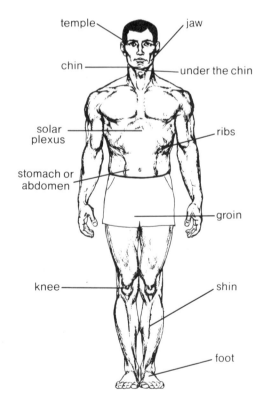

3. Use a combination of techniques. A single blow or *takedown* (a move in which the aggressor is thrown to the ground) may end a fight, but do not count on it. Always plan ahead and know what to do next. For example, a high punch followed by a takedown may end the fight. If the punch does not stop your opponent or is blocked, the throw can still end the confrontation. Each technique should lead to the next, forming a strong combination for self-defense.

4. Keep your opponent confused. Try not to let the aggressor predict your next move. Confusion leads to worry, which causes mistakes. Keep your opponent mentally off balance by distractions and movement. Gesture, yell, or throw something to divert attention from the techniques you plan to use. For example, you may make a gesture with one hand to distract your opponent, while launching an attack with the other hand. Movement is another way to keep an opponent guessing. Many great fighters move almost continually to keep their opponents off balance and to set them up for attack. Practice distraction techniques with a partner so that you are ready for a real fight.

5. Be persistent. Do not give up even if your opponent seems to be winning. The other person may appear strong, but may still be far more tired than you. One strong punch or takedown

might turn the fight in your favor. Persistence is one of the signs of a winner.

## 5. Do I need physical conditioning in order to be good at Western self-protection techniques?

Any student of a fighting art should spend at least a part of each day doing calisthenics to loosen and stretch the body. Also, certain strengthening exercises may be useful. It is recommended that students combine calisthenics, strengthening exercises, and endurance-building activities. Before working out, always warm up sufficiently to prepare your body for training. After training, do a series of stretches again to cool your body down. Recommended exercises are explained in the next chapter.

## 6. Do I need any equipment to train for self-protection?

Anyone who wants to train in Western self-defense should practice techniques in front of a mirror in order to develop proper form. This is often called *shadowboxing*. You should also practice blows on a heavy punching bag in order to develop power, speed, and form. Punching air is not the same as hitting a bag. Other supplementary equipment such as a jump rope is very good for speed and endurance. When you practice with a partner you should wear a mouthpiece, protective head gear, and protective gloves. Males should wear a groin cup. When practicing grappling, always use a thick, wrestling-type mat. It is suggested that before you purchase any equipment, you first learn how to use it at a health club or school under the supervision of an instructor. This insures

that you will use it correctly and safely if you later choose to purchase it, and that you will know whether you like it before you buy it.

## 7. What is the best way to begin self-protection training?

I always strongly recommend that an interested person find a self-defense instructor who explains things well, enjoys working with beginners, and is safety-conscious. A book can never replace a good teacher, it can only be an extra guide for students.

In practice sessions, students should not actually hit their partners. Stop any blows approximately one inch (2.5 centimeters) from the other person. Students should be careful not to use full force in punching and grappling. The emphasis in practice is on developing proper form, movement, and timing—not on having an actual fight.

Students who wear safety equipment, practice under proper supervision, and are careful, usually enjoy practice and learn a great deal.

## 8. Are hand techniques different in Western self-defense than in Oriental fighting arts?

In Western self-defense, the closed fist is used in all hand techniques. The basic blows are usually the left jab, the right straight punch, left hook, right hook, and uppercut. When properly executed, these punches are effective enough for most situations. In Oriental forms of fighting, the fist, open hand, finger combinations, the elbow, and the forearm are used in attacking techniques. The great variety of techniques offered in Eastern self-defense provides tremendous flexibility in defenses, but is not always necessary in dealing with an ordinary bully.

## 9. Are punching techniques better than kicks?

In a fight, an average person will probably use hands more readily than feet for defense. An effective foot fighter must condition the legs and develop proper kicking technique. It is probably wise to use kicks for fighting at a long distance, punches at a medium distance, and grappling for close distances. If a person is not highly flexible and does not want to spend time developing foot techniques, then punching techniques along with grappling will make up a practical arsenal for self-defense.

## 10. What are the best blows in the Western tradition for ordinary self-defense?

Probably the most effective punches for beginners are the left jab and the right straight punch. A one-two combination of these can be extremely powerful. The jab sets up and weakens the opponent. The right straight punch has the power to end a fight.

## 11. Can a small person pack as much punch as a bigger person?

Physical conditioning and skill help develop power. The individual who uses proper leverage and technique can sometimes generate more force than someone bigger who is unskilled. That is why good martial artists must not only condition themselves to a peak, but also work on the proper form of execution of the techniques.

## 12. How can you combine strategy with knowledge of the areas of the body that you should strike?

The main target areas in wrestling and boxing are sensitive enough that a hit to one of them can take the fight out of an opponent without usually doing any permanent damage. These main areas are the face, under the chin, jaw, solar plexus, and the stomach. In a real fight it may be necessary to adjust your aim slightly from these targets. Under the right circumstances, it is often wise to stamp on an attacker's foot or kick the person's shins. When you are in extreme danger, it may even be advisable to hit a very sensitive area such as the knee or groin. Obviously, which target you choose will depend a lot on where there is an opening. It is important to not only hit the right target but to generate maximum power through proper technique. A powerful blow to the stomach may effectively end a fight even though the stomach is not the most sensitive area on the body. You can often win by consistently hitting one target until the opponent weakens.

Remember, it isn't how many punches you know, but how well you can execute those that you have learned. A good one-two punch can end any fight by itself.

# 2

# PHYSICAL CONDITIONING

As a beginning self-defense student, you should avoid stretching your muscles too much at any given practice session. It is far better to stretch slowly, day by day, than to risk injuring your muscles.

Below are a few basic stretching and conditioning exercises around which you can build your own warm-up and conditioning program.

## Basic Side Stretch

Stand erect with your feet about ten inches (25 centimeters) apart. Place your left hand on your hip and reach and stretch with your right hand as far to your left as you can. Straighten up and then stretch to the other side. Stretch to each side three times.

## Toe Touch

Stand erect with your feet slightly apart and your arms hanging loosely at your sides. Reach both arms above your head, then reach down and try to touch the ground. Keep your legs nearly straight, but reach down only until your muscles resist. Don't force it. Repeat ten times.

21

## Basic Wall Push-Up

Place the palms of your hands against a solid object and move your feet at least three feet (about 1 meter) away from it. Bend your elbows, bringing your chest close to the object. Hold that position for at least a count of twenty-five.

## Basic Two-Leg Stretch

Stand erect with your feet spread slightly apart. Slowly spread your legs as far apart as possible without straining the muscles. Increase the amount of spread with every practice session. Do this only once during each exercise session.

# 3

# THE FOUNDATION OF DEFENSE: STANCE AND MOVEMENT

The first lesson in your development as a fighter is *stance* or body position. You must develop correct body position as a foundation for withstanding attacks and mounting counterattacks. It is important to be balanced and steady even when moving. An attacker could take advantage of any instability you show during movement.

In Western self-protection, movement is very important. It allows you to avoid an attacker's blows, places you in a position to strike, and keeps an attacker guessing what you are going to do. It is also important because a still target is the easiest to hit. Try to move in a relaxed position throughout a fight. Students of self-defense should practice their fighting stance (position) and movement daily.

If you are fortunate enough to have a heavy bag to work with, then move around it, imagining it is your opponent. First, do each movement slowly, and then gradually speed it up. After you have enough confidence in your ability to do a particular movement, combine it with another. When you can do different combinations of movement at various speeds, you are ready to try combining them with fighting techniques, such as punches. An excellent fighter is one who uses movement not only for defense, but as a positive weapon in his or her arsenal.

Practice your movements combined with fighting techniques and by themselves. While practicing movement, try to imagine that you are dealing with an attacker. Unlike certain Oriental martial arts, Western self-defense techniques do not teach that you must meet the opponent head-on. They allow you to circle an opponent and attack from the side or even from behind with grappling techniques.

---

## BASIC STANCE

To assume the basic stance, stand with your left foot forward, toe turned slightly inward. Your right foot should rest on the ball of the foot, with the heel aproximately two inches (4 centimeters) off the ground. Your left arm

is carried high—at chin level—and your shoulders are relaxed. Your left hand is made into a fist with the thumb folded over. Your right hand is held under your ear, with the palm facing slightly forward. Keep your elbows close to your ribs to protect them. Tuck your chin down toward the breastbone. Your whole body should feel strong, yet relaxed enough to quickly unleash an attack. Whenever possible, try to position yourself so that your forward foot is on a line running between the attacker's feet. The left leg is usually the forward leg for right-handed people. (If you are left-handed you may want to reverse this stance to keep your powerful left hand in the rear. All of the descriptions and illustrations have the left foot forward and the right foot in the rear.)

NOTE: A variation of the stance allows you to stand more erectly and keep both heels flat on the floor.

## STEPPING TECHNIQUES

### Slide Step

The basic movement is the slide step. First the left foot moves, then the back foot slides forward. To move backward, reverse the procedure. Move the back foot first, and then the forward foot.

### Side Step

To sidestep the attacker to the left, you most commonly move the left foot first, and then the right foot. If you want to move to the right, move the right foot first. Continual practice with this basic movement will teach a certain skill and gracefulness. This technique is often combined with the up-and-down, side-to-side, and front-to-rear upper body movement described later in the chapter.

## Fast Advance

This is a slight modification of the basic slide step that covers greater distance more quickly. The technique is initiated by the left foot lifting slightly off the ground as you push off with the right rear leg. One foot should be in contact with the ground at all times.

## The Circling Movement

This method of movement lets you maintain your body position while circling around your attacker. It allows you to avoid your attacker's blows, keep your attacker confused, and attack your adversary from an angle.

To circle an attacker, move the forward foot four to eight inches (10 to 20 centimeters) in the direction you want to move. Once your advancing foot has moved into place, use it as a pivot to swing the rest of the body in the desired direction. When the pivot is complete, make sure that the rear foot is planted firmly on the ground. After completing this two-step maneuver you should again be in a strong fighting stance.

NOTE: The model took his first step to the right with his left foot and used that foot to pivot the rest of his body to the right.

## UPPER BODY MOVEMENT

In addition to movement started with the feet, there is upper body motion. This motion may be up-and-down, side-to-side, or front-to-rear. These movements can be done while standing still or while moving the feet. By using these upper body movements, you can confuse your opponent, make yourself a harder target to hit, and evade blows.

Beginning students should first develop a strong, stable stance and combine it with foot movement before trying to include upper body motion in their practice. Once you feel confident of your ability to take a strong position and move with it, try shifting your head and shoulders up and down, as though avoiding punches. Next, practice bending your knees deeply as you bend forward at the waist. Once these up-and-down body movements are comfortable, try bending the top half of your body to one side, then the other. This side-to-side movement can be used to fake out an opponent and avoid certain attacks. Then practice bending to the rear from your waist, as though to move back from a blow. When these actions feel natural, try to use them with different movements of the feet. While performing any upper body movement, keep your eyes on the aggressor and be ready to further defend or attack. In real confrontations, various upper body movements flow together in what seems to be almost one continuous motion.

If an opponent throws a left jab, it can be avoided by bending slightly sideward. The second attack of a right straight punch misses when the defender bends deeply downward. Upper body movement goes together with the evasion skills taught in a later chapter to prepare you for self-protection. The better you are at avoiding contact with an opponent's attack, the greater your chances to prevail.

# 4

# THE ART OF PUNCHING

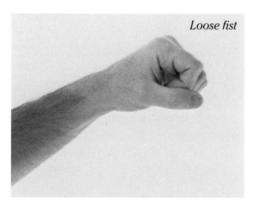

*Loose fist*

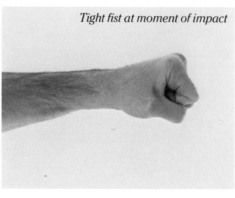

*Tight fist at moment of impact*

Punching techniques have developed over many hundreds of years. Each punch has its advantages and its disadvantages and you must learn to use the best technique for a particular situation. Whenever you are throwing a punch, it is important to make sure that it is thrown from the body and not merely from the shoulder. Twist your body while the punch is thrown to put the whole body behind the blow. If you put all of your body weight into a punch, you may generate more power than a far stronger individual who simply depends on arm strength. The fist must extend outward so that it hits at the same time as the hip and the shoulder are turned forward. Make sure that after a hit, your hand is retracted into a cocked position. When throwing a punch, the arm and fist should be loose until just before impact. At the last second, the fist should be tightened as though squeezing a ball. In this way the punch is fast, yet the hand is tight and not easily hurt when hitting the target.

## Left Jab

Learning how to handle distance is a very important part of self-defense. At times you may want to close in on an opponent in order to execute a power punch or to grapple. You will not always be able to simply rush in. The left jab is an excellent technique to use while closing distance with your opponent. This punch can also create an opening for your next move when your opponent tries to block it. It is probably the best lead technique in Western self-defense.

A jab is not a knock-out punch and should be used to keep the attacker off balance. It has the advantage of being repeatable because of its speed. Often a jab is used at two different heights to set up the opponent. For example, the left punch is first thrown to the opponent's body to lower his or her guard and then launched again to the head. A quick series of jabs should immediately be followed with an attack from the right arm. The left jab can also be an effective block for an aggressor's right straight punch.

To execute a jab, turn your left fist a quarter turn as you launch it from the shoulder. At the moment of impact the knuckles will be on top. While jabbing with your left hand, your right hand should be relaxed, in position, and ready to guard against a counterattack. Make sure to throw your jab not just *at* the target, but *through* it. Open your right hand and bring it in front of your face to catch your opponent's counterattack.

## Right Straight Punch

A combination of factors makes the right straight punch a very powerful weapon. It is thrown from the rear hand, so it gains your whole body weight behind it as it shoots forward. For most people, the right hand is the strongest, and this also contributes to the technique's force. It is a useful follow-up technique for the left jab.

To perform the right straight punch, shift your body weight onto the front (left) leg as your rear hip and shoulder turn forward. While turning, throw your right arm toward the target. At the moment of impact your fist should be turned so that the knuckles are on top and the side of the fist is turned outward. Keep your body loose until a split second before impact, when your fist should be squeezed tight. While delivering the punch, bring your left arm across your body to act as a guard against counterattack.

It is generally best to aim this attack at the opponent's head, because a punch to the body would allow the aggressor to throw a jab at your face.

## Left Hook

This powerhouse punch can easily catch a bully by surprise. Body action must be correct and timing perfect to get the proper benefit from the technique. This is not a punch that you should use to lead an attack. It is used either as a follow-up to another technique, or as a counter after avoiding an aggressor's attack.

To execute this technique, lean forward slightly from the waist. Turn your left hip and shoulder to the right while bringing your left arm around in a hooking motion. Your arm should be loose until the split second before impact. On impact the thumb side of your fist should be facing upward. As you deliver your left hook, bring your right hand into position to block any follow-up by your opponent.

## Uppercut

This blow takes little room to deliver, making it extremely useful at close range. Launch your fist, palm facing upward, so that your knuckles make contact with your opponent's body. This technique can be used effectively with either hand. Bend your knees before the punch, and drive upward with your legs to put power behind your arm as it shoots toward the target. Springing up and turning the hip into the uppercut gives it a great deal of power.

## Right Hook

This punch can be quite useful when delivered properly at close range. To execute the technique, shift your weight onto the forward leg while you turn your right hip forward. Keep your elbows in tight to protect your ribs. As your right shoulder comes even with your left, your right arm shoots out in a short arc. Your fist hits with the thumb side facing upward. The key to gaining power in this technique is the pivoting of the body.

# 5

# KICKING TECHNIQUES

Kicking is not as easy as it seems in the movies. Each kicking technique must be practiced many times before it becomes a practical weapon for defense.

Kicking, like other fighting techniques, has both advantages and disadvantages. One disadvantage of kicking is that a kick is sometimes easy to spot and block. Also, if a kick is executed slowly or at too high a level, an attacker can more easily throw the kicker off balance. The two main advantages of kicking are power and range: the human leg, because of its great strength, is able to deliver a powerful blow; and a kick, because of the leg's length, has considerable range.

Because of the advantages and disadvantages of every technique, a good self-defense student will try to combine techniques. A student who is effective at kicking, punching, and grappling, is effective at any range and will have a defense for any situation.

## Knee Kick

The knee kick is used for striking an aggressor who is standing close in front of you. It is an effective technique for striking the stomach or groin of an attacker. To execute the technique, bring your knee up sharply and hit the aggressor in the stomach or groin.

## Basic Front Kick

The front kick is a powerful foot technique used for counterattack. It is used most often to strike an aggressor's shins, knees, groin, chest, or head. To execute the kick, bend the knee of your kicking leg and lift it toward your chest. Turn the toes upward so they will not be injured when your foot hits the target. Snap the kicking leg forward and hit the target with the ball of your foot.

NOTE: The stamping kick is a variation of the front kick used to strike an opponent's knees, shins, or feet. When your opponent grabs you from the front, raise the bent knee of your kicking leg and thrust that leg out and down so that your heel strikes the opponent's knee, shin, or foot. The stamping kick is an excellent means of distracting your opponent's attention long enough for you to throw a punch without being blocked.

# 6

# HOW TO AVOID BEING HIT: DODGES AND BLOCKS

The two basic ways to avoid harm in Western self-protection are evasions, or dodges, and blocks. Balance and body position are important in both of these. This chapter will teach you evasions and blocks, along with some simple counterattacks which can slow down your opponent or end the fight.

## DODGING

Western self-defense includes strong evasion techniques. These dodges are often referred to as slipping because, when a punch is thrown, you slip away from it. Slipping has the distinct advantage of keeping the attacker's punch from coming into contact with you, so you don't use energy in a block. When you block, you absorb a certain amount of power from your opponent. This can eventually wear you out. In slipping, it is very important to keep your balance. When you slip properly, the attacker will not only miss, but leave an opening for a counterattack.

## Slipping to the Side

If the attacker throws a left jab, move your head to the outside of the attacker's punch. Then throw a right straight punch to counter. This slipping technique is a common type of side-to-side movement.

## Circle Dodge

If the attacker rushes forward, you may avoid him or her by a circle dodge. This involves stepping away from the aggressor and then pivoting to bring yourself back into a proper stance facing in a new direction, a distance from the attack. This is a variation of the circling movement. Immediately follow through with a counterattack of your own.

## Downward Dodge

If an aggressor throws a punch with his or her right arm, dodge downward by crouching beneath the punch. Follow with an attack to the middle of the attacker's body. This is an example of an up-and-down movement that can be used to avoid a blow.

## BLOCKING

It is very important that you do not just rely on block after block or show too much pride in your ability to avoid being hit. This would reveal your inability to counterattack, and would encourage your attacker to continue moving in with blows. If you only block and dodge, your attacker will eventually wear you down and penetrate your defenses. For this reason alone, you must get used to following up each block with a counterblow of your own.

### High Block

If an aggressor throws a punch toward your face, simply raise the closest arm so that it blocks the aggressor's punch. Immediately after blocking, you should follow through with a counterattack.

Do not leave too much time lag between your block and counter. If you do not *immediately* counterattack after blocking, the aggressor will have time to hit you with another punch.

## Medium Block

When an attacker throws a punch at your body, bring the arm closest to the attack across your body, so that it meets the attacker's limb. Then throw a counterpunch with your other hand. It is often preferable to grab the aggressor's arm after blocking it, in order to keep it tied up while you throw your own punch.

## Low Block

When an attacker launches a blow toward your stomach or groin, swing the arm closest to the attack down and across your body until it meets the blow. After your arm meets the attacker's limb, continue the movement to sweep the attack away from you. Be sure not to reach out to block an attack. Instead, try to meet and deflect the attack while properly balanced. Once the blow is stopped, immobilize the limb by opening your fist and grabbing the opponent. This should give you a brief opening for your counterattack.

## Blocking Kicks

Generally it is better to dodge kicks than to block them. This is because of their power and reach. Sometimes a block may be absolutely necessary, such as when the aggressor throws a front kick. To block such an attack, simply lower your arm as if you were blocking a punch.

After blocking, you may grab the aggressor's leg and take him or her down. To do so, move your body in close to your opponent. Bend your head forward and press your shoulders tightly against the aggressor. Lock your leg behind the attacker's leg, and kick the person's legs out from underneath him or her.

## Parrying

Parrying is redirecting an aggressor's attack. It can be done with either hand in a variety of positions. You parry by moving your open hand to brush the attacking arm away. Your hand should cross the aggressor's wrist. Move your elbow only as much as necessary.

Before parrying, decide where you want the opponent's attacking arm to end up. If you want it to end up on the outside so that the person cannot easily counterattack, sweep the arm away so that it crosses the opponent's body. This will make it difficult for the attacker's other arm to reach you. If, however, you want to create an opening along the center line of the attacker's body, sweep your opponent's arm outward. Protect your body with your non-punching arm, or grab the attacker's arm, so that he or she cannot hit you. Follow up after a parry by countering with your other hand.

# 7

# COMBINATIONS

One blow may not stop the attacker, but a series of well-executed punches will often do the job. A good self-defense technician learns how to put together combinations of techniques. First, practice individual techniques, and then try to work them into a pattern together so that one move flows to the next.

Do not continually repeat the same techniques. If you repeat the same fighting techniques over and over in the same order, the attacker will soon figure out a strategy to penetrate your defenses.

You will find that if you lead with a left, you will want to follow through with a right; if you punch high the first time, you can punch lower next time with the same arm. In this way, you can vary the pattern of your attack so that it is difficult for the opponent to know what to expect.

When you are attacking, watch your opponent's reaction so that you can adjust your strategy. For example, if you plan to use a one-two combination (left jab then right straight punch) but the opponent evades your jab, adjust by throwing a different follow-up attack.

If practiced regularly, the strong combinations which follow can be quite effective. You can also create your own combinations. Remember that hand techniques without efficient footwork are greatly weakened. You will not be able to penetrate a skilled defense unless you move your feet in conjunction with your hand techniques. Always practice the various punches from a stationary position and as you move.

## Left Jab, Right Straight Punch

A simple one-two of left jab, right straight punch is a very effective combination. As an attacker moves forward, lead with a left jab. If the jab doesn't stop the attacker or the person blocks, bring your arm back into position while turning your right hip forward to deliver a right straight punch.

## Left Jab, Right Straight Punch, Left Hook

When a simple one-two combination doesn't stop an attacker or the person tries to block your right straight punch, twist your body back so your right arm returns to the rear position while you throw a left hook. This three-way combination is very effective in working from one side of the body to the other to develop power.

## Left Jab, Right Hook, Left Uppercut

First throw a left jab. If an attacker blocks it or a second blow is needed, bring your left arm back into position while twisting your right hip forward. As your hip moves, shoot your right arm out in a hook. Immediately upon impact of the punch, twist your hips back as you shoot a left uppercut into the opponent's ribs.

## Front Kick, Left Jab, Right Straight Punch

This is a very good combination for moving from a distance to close range. First, slide your rear leg forward as your front leg lifts and coils. Snap your foot hard to the attacker's knee or groin. Be sure to curl your toes up away from the blow and connect with the ball of the foot. Immediately follow up with a left jab and then a right straight punch.

## Left Jab, Left Jab, Right Straight Punch

When faced off against an aggressive bully, keep the person at a distance with a couple of quick jabs. When the opponent appears to be committed to protecting one part of his or her body against those jabs, follow through with a right straight punch to an unprotected area.

### Right Uppercut, Left Hook, Right Straight Punch, Right Knee

This quick series is very useful if you are close to an opponent. If your opponent leaves you an opening in the stomach or solar plexus, drive your right fist toward it. After contact, recoil your right arm at the same time as your left hook shoots out to the side of the opponent's head. Follow up with a right straight punch to a high area of the body. If necessary to end the fight, the right knee can be driven up hard to the attacker's groin.

# 8

# COMBINING BOXING AND GRAPPLING

If the attacker is not as strong or as skillful at grappling as you, closing in quickly and grabbing the person might be a good tactic. If you are small and weak, you must have at least a basic knowledge of wrestling skills so that if you are forced in close, you will not be helpless.

Some basic principles will help you in any grappling situation. Make sure that an opponent's balance is broken before attempting to throw him or her. This will make your throw easier to perform, because an opponent who is off balance will find it difficult to use his or her strength to stop you. Sometimes the aggressor will break his or her own balance simply by making the first move. For example, bullies who push you backward will usually put their weight on the balls of their feet. They can easily be thrown forward because their balance is broken in that direction. Aggressors who try to pull you forward usually fall off balance to the rear and can therefore be thrown backward easily.

There are situations, however, when an attacker's balance is not broken even though he or she has made an aggressive move. In these situations, if you choose to grapple you must first break the bully's balance by pushing or pulling the person before attempting a throw. In the throws shown in this chapter, disrupting the opponent's balance is usually done during the first two or three steps of the technique.

When you are learning to knock an opponent off balance, it is best to practice on a mat with a fellow student. When grappling keep the following helpful points in mind.

1. Always watch an opponent's stance carefully. You should attempt your throw at the exact moment when he or she is off balance.
2. Keep your body loose at all times, so that you can respond quickly when you see your opponent is off balance.
3. Remember that an aggressor is always easiest to throw in the direction in which he or she is moving.

4. If an opponent is not off balance, you can break the person's balance by directing his or her energy to your own advantage. If your opponent pushes, you should pull. If he or she pulls, then you should push. If an opponent is close and attempts to grab you, side-step and sweep the person's arms in the direction he or she is pulling or pushing. The opponent's momentum will destabilize him or her so you can avoid the attack or sometimes even throw the person.

## DEFENSES FROM THE GROUND

Sometimes you may be thrown and forced to defend yourself from the ground. Usually it is best to get up as soon as possible, unless you are an extremely good grappler. The defenses listed here are for times when you are unable to get up quickly. They follow a sequence similar to what might be encountered in a real fight. They may, however, differ from what you would see in sport wrestling. You should develop the ability to do maneuvers very quickly and to flexibly adapt them to the circumstances. When practicing ground work, it is advisable to do it on a mat, to use knee pads, and to have proper supervision.

## The Lever Leg Lift Throw

If you are forced down toward the ground, and you are on one knee facing your aggressor, turn slightly so that your chest faces the side of the opponent. Reach down behind the opponent's closest leg and grasp it from behind the ankle. Rest your other forearm right above the opponent's kneecap. Press down on the opponent's leg as you lift up behind his or her ankle while starting to stand. The combination of actions should throw the opponent backward. Be very careful in practice not to put heavy pressure with your forearm on the area of the knee. Instead, practice the technique slowly, with only light pressure on the upper leg, two inches (5 centimeters) above the area by the knee that you would press in a real fight.

## The Basic Bicycle Kick

If you are thrown onto your back and the opponent is rushing toward you, the easiest defense is a bicycle kick. Many bullies do not expect their victims to keep on fighting once they have been thrown to the ground, so they are easily caught off guard by such a technique. When the attacker moves toward you while you are on the ground, position your body so that your feet are aimed at him or her. As the person moves toward you, thrust one leg and then the other toward the shin, knee, or groin. Your legs should move as if you were bicycling. Do not try to stand until the attacker has retreated. Ready your hands for punching in the event that your foot defense is not successful.

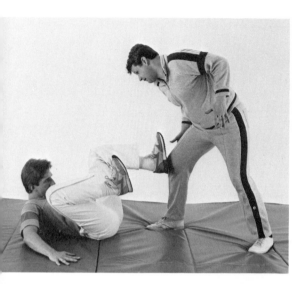

## The Pull Down from the Front

If both you and the aggressor are forced onto the ground facing one another, you must take immediate advantage of the situation by breaking the person's balance and taking him or her down. One of the ways to do this is to push backward. Usually the aggressor will counter by pushing forward against you. As he or she does, pull forward. Bend the person's head down against your chest, and slide your arms down around your opponent to lock the person into position. Next, quickly turn around to the person's side as you pull his or her arm down and toward you, forcing the person onto his or her back. Be sure to push with your chest for added leverage as you pull down on the arm. Once you have the opponent on his or her back, free one of your hands and finish with a punch. Several variations of this type of maneuver can be used in grappling. If you are familiar with wrestling techniques then adapt the appropriate maneuver to your needs.

## The Side Force-Down with Arm Lever

If you and your opponent are on the ground side by side, quickly reach one arm around the person's waist as you grab the arm closest to you. Put your head against his or her armpit as you push forward and force the arm backward. This should throw the opponent to the ground face first. Once your opponent is on the ground, you may turn his or her arm so that the palm is facing up. Pull up on the wrist and push down on the back of the opponent's elbow, applying pressure to the joint to lock his or her arm.

There is a simple variation of this. Grasp the far arm and flip the person onto his or her back. Free one hand and follow up with a punch.

## Escape from a Pin on the Ground

If the opponent has trapped you on your back with both hands pinned, arch your back while you lift your pelvis upward. As the attacker moves forward, free one of your arms and drive it up hard into the opponent's groin. To throw the person off you, twist your body to the side as you push him or her in the same direction.

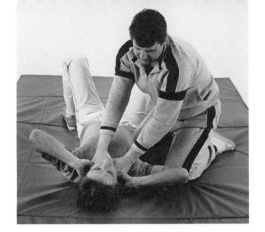

## Escape from a Choke on the Ground

If an attacker tries to choke you from the side, grab the person's little fingers. Lift the fingers up and outward. Next jam the knee closest to the opponent into his or her ribs. At the same time, push forward while pulling outward against the person's little fingers to throw him or her backward to the ground. In a real confrontation, if you snap your opponent's little fingers outward very hard you may end the fight because of the pain that it causes your opponent. If necessary, finish with a punch.

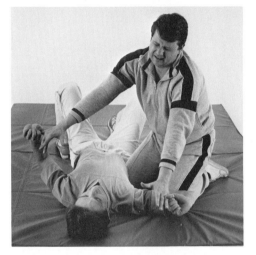

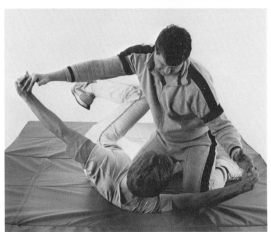

## DEFENSES WHILE STANDING

### Single Leg Pick-Up and Sweep

If an attacker throws a punch, duck underneath it. Slide in close to the opponent, placing your forward leg between the person's legs. Lift up on your opponent's forward ankle while sweeping his or her other foot out from under.

## Double Leg Takedown

When you get in close to an attacker and he or she attempts to push your body down so that you cannot punch, reach down and grab the backs of both of his or her legs. Drive down and forward with your shoulders against the person's body while pulling his or her legs up and out.

## Outside Sweep

If your opponent pulls you forward, slide your leg to the outside of your opponent's. Then grab his or her arm while pushing backward against the person's opposite shoulder. At the same time, sweep your leg behind you to throw the aggressor off his or her feet.

A variation is to push back on the opponent's chin while sweeping his or her leg out from under.

## Fireman's Carry

When an attacker closes in or is resting his or her weight on your shoulder, the fireman's carry can be effective. Bend downward and reach between the person's legs. Get a firm grip on the back of the opponent's right leg while pulling down on his or her right arm. Straighten up and throw the opponent over your shoulder by bending slightly to the side.

## Left Jab, Outside Sweep

After you throw a jab, if your opponent closes in, step outside his or her leg with your forward foot. Then grab the person's nearest arm while pushing backward against his or her chin with your other hand. Make sure your rear leg is behind the opponent's leg. At the same time, sweep your leg behind you to throw the aggressor off his or her feet.

# 9

# STRATEGY

Many people think of fighting as simply overpowering an opponent. In reality, the winner of a fight is not necessarily the stronger person. The winner is often the individual who best handles strategy. Even people with massive physiques have limitations on their strength, but the mind's power is almost limitless. A small person who uses his or her mind can overpower a giant who relies on physical attributes. The great boxing champion Bob Fitzimmons once said, "The bigger they are, the heavier they fall." This advice comes from a man who held three titles: the middleweight, light heavyweight, and heavyweight championships of the world. What Fitzimmons knew is that the fighter who can out-think his opponent always has the advantage.

This chapter is designed to help you develop a fighting strategy that will give you an edge over any opponent. This does not mean, however, that you should ignore other aspects of fighting, such as physical conditioning, technique, distancing, speed, and timing. Rather, it means a person who has developed all of these other factors can learn to best use his or her skills and to exploit the weaknesses of an opponent through proper strategy.

Every opponent will be unique in some way. The ability to recognize and adjust to an opponent's fighting characteristics is the trait of a winner. Beginning students of self-protection should concentrate on carefully learning and applying basic strategy.

# GENERAL STRATEGIC PRINCIPLES

There are specific strategic concerns that must be kept in mind in almost all physical confrontations. A short discussion of these general concerns follows, along with suggestions on how to best apply them in a confrontation.

## 1. Control the situation.

It is paramount that you control the situation as much as possible. Do not let a bully determine how, where, and when a fight is going to begin. When an aggressive individual confronts you, first size up your location. Do not allow yourself to be placed in a corner where you cannot easily escape, unless you are far stronger than your opponent and feel comfortable that your grappling skills would enable you to prevail.

Once it is clear that your opponent intends to fight, keep your eyes on your opponent's. Be careful to see that he or she does not reach for a weapon or an object to strike you with. Be ready for a sneak attack. For example, do not take your coat off while your opponent waits to fight you. Never turn your back on an opponent once that person has shown a willingness to fight. If you are in a strange place, do not walk out a back door or into a dark room or an alley where you easily could be caught off guard.

Seize the initiative by taking a comfortable, well-balanced stance so you are ready for quick action. Often, if you are prepared for the battle, your opponent will sense your determination and back off.

Do not allow the bully to take control by upsetting you with verbal assaults. Instead, make it clear through both your expression and your words that what he or she is saying doesn't affect you.

Concentrate on what is taking place and not on how you would feel if you were hurt. Size up your opponent's skill and determination so you can plan your strategy and be better prepared after the fight has started. One way to do this is by faking a punch or a blow. If your opponent instinctively picks up his or her leg to throw a kick, then you will know you are facing a kicker; on the other hand, if the person widens his or her stance and moves his or her fists, your opponent prefers punching.

## 2. Consider distancing.

Watch the distance between you and your opponent. There are four fighting distances in Western self-defense: safety range, long range, close range, and grappling range. *Safety range* is the distance at which neither you nor your opponent can reach the other with a blow. *Long range* is the distance at which you can hit the aggressor with certain lead hand or foot attacks. Techniques such as the front kick or left jab are usually used at this range.

*Close range* is reserved for shorter punching techniques, such as hooks or uppercuts. At *grappling range,* you are so close to your opponent that you can apply throws or holds.

*Close range*

*Safety range*

*Grappling range*

*Long range*

It is very important to think in terms of these ranges when you are in a fight, so that you choose the right distance at the proper time to take advantage of your opponent's strengths or weaknesses. Make your opponent fight the opposite type of fight from what he or she is good at. For example, if your opponent is a grappler, make him or her box from a distance. Plan your strategy carefully, and time your actions so that you do not come within range of the opponent's attack and can hit the person when he or she is vulnerable. Make it hard to hit you with power.

If you are better at grappling techniques, try to stay close to the aggressor so you can grab the person and take him or her down. If you prefer punching or kicking, try to keep the appropriate distance between you and the opponent for these techniques to be useful. In general, it is a good idea to stand out of reach of an aggressor. This will force the aggressor to move toward you in order to attack, and this movement will give you extra time to react.

A person with little self-defense experience often stands too close to an opponent. If you are shorter than your opponent, this can be very dangerous. The taller aggressor will have greater reach and may be able to disable you with a quick attack before you can mount a defense. Once a fight starts, try to make the opponent stay at a distance at which his or her best fighting techniques cannot easily be used.

You can close the gap between you and your opponent by throwing either a lead technique or a fake accompanied by a fast movement forward. However, never make a half-hearted effort; instead, commit yourself in a smooth, even movement. Move around to keep the ideal distance between you and your opponent: the range at which you can take advantage of your strengths, yet your opponent finds it difficult to do likewise.

## 3. Take advantage of movement.

Move to slip away from an attack, to set an aggressor up for an angle attack, and to frustrate the opponent. Keep your eyes on the attacker and when he or she moves, take advantage of any opening.

Try not to remain stationary once the fight begins. If an aggressor enters the range of your blows, be sure to throw a punch. Try to keep your opponent confused by a series of moves coupled with hand techniques. While moving, make sure to stay balanced at all times.

Whenever your opponent gets set to throw a punch, move out of the way. If you time your movement properly, your opponent will be thrown off balance, possibly leaving an opening for counterattack.

## 4. Use hand and foot techniques properly and in combinations.

While you move, keep your hands high and loose. When you are tense, your reaction time is slower and you tire more quickly.

Never rely on just a block-and-punch combination. Confuse the aggressor by a variety of hand and foot combinations, so that he or she will not be able to figure out a strategy to overcome you. Do not just keep aiming for the same spot on the opponent. Try to throw techniques at high, middle, and low targets to keep the opponent from anticipating your moves. If your opponent appears to be weakening because of sensitivity on one part of the body, draw the person's attention away from that spot with attacks or fakes to another area and then catch him or her with follow-up blows to the sensitive spot. Once you are inside the opponent's guard position (at close range), throw a quick series of punches. If necessary, move in to grappling range and try a lock or throw. If you don't move in to grappling range after a series of punches, move quickly away from the bully.

Punch only when there is an opening. Do not just throw punches to do something or hope that they will hit a sensitive spot on the attacker. You must aim for a specific target and commit yourself to it. Otherwise you will be wasting energy and hitting parts of the attacker that will not easily weaken him or her.

# HANDLING FIGHTERS OF DIFFERENT SIZES AND STRENGTHS

Sometimes you may be smaller and weaker than your opponent. At other times, you may be the larger and stronger. Your strategy depends on the person you are up against. However, even though a comparison of size and strength is very useful, it should not be the only basis for your strategy. Some people use a different fighting technique than you would expect from someone of their size and strength. Adjust your strategy accordingly.

This section discusses handling fighters of different body types, and the next section will discuss how to handle particular styles of fighters. Your ability to assess the type of person you are up against, develop a plan, and commit yourself to the appropriate action will determine your chances of coming out on top.

A breakdown of strategies to handle the different body types of attackers follows.

## Taller and More Powerful Attacker

When fighting a larger opponent, you most likely have an advantage of speed. Use this advantage by continually moving and drawing your opponent's attacks. Make the attacker throw a long punch (such as a jab) so that he or she leaves an opening for a counterattack. Immediately after your opponent tries any technique, throw a

series of fast punches at any openings. Then quickly move away and regroup at a safe distance. Do not stay close to your opponent after punching, unless he or she is clearly off balance and you are absolutely positive that you have far superior grappling abilities.

Whenever possible, attack at an angle to your opponent, hitting the ribs or other targets from the side. If you are not in front of your opponent, it will be much harder for him or her to counterattack. Keep moving around your opponent, and wait for an opening; then move in very fast. Do not become impatient. Allow your opponent to make mistakes or create openings. If your opponent charges, dodge or move to the side, and then counter-attack. Even a very powerful opponent will have difficulty hitting you with full force when off balance.

Be careful not to put yourself where your opponent can easily grab you. If the opponent comes very close, push the person away, kick at his or her shins, or use your knees to get space to maneuver. Take control of the fighting space with your movement so you cannot be cornered. Try to stay at the edge of the safety range whenever you are not actually hitting your opponent.

When you are shorter and weaker than your opponent, it is necessary to fight conservatively by only moving fast when he or she is close in range. Circling the opponent at a distance while slowly wearing the person down should be a part of any plan. Be cautious if your opponent starts to slow down his or her attacks. Sometimes this can be a trick to bring you in toward the person. Remember the goal is self-defense, not scoring a dramatic win. Test the situation by a short attack at the opponent's side, and then quickly retreat at an angle. If the opponent is truly weakened, pick a sensitive spot and go after it whenever attacking. Try not to let a weakened opponent rest. Keep him or her moving or defending from surprise attacks.

The general strategy for an opponent like this is to wear the person down with angle attacks until you can finish him or her off or your opponent gets discouraged and quits.

## Taller and Weaker Attacker

A taller and weaker opponent will often try to take advantage or his or her longer reach and hit you from a distance. Stay out of range of this opponent's punches until you are ready to attack. Dodge and keep low so that you present a smaller target. Watch carefully to see if there is any hesitation between your opponent's punches. Try to dodge blows and move in with speedy attacks of your own while the opponent hesitates. When attacking, try to slip inside your opponent's guard to punch to the body. Use forceful blows to the side of the opponent's body until a clear opening is available.

If the opponent doesn't leave clear openings, draw out a punch by pretending to move in toward the person. Then sidestep that punch and move in close with a combination of punches.

determined and your opponent will lose confidence and the desire to fight.

When you are shorter and more powerful than your opponent, try to encourage him or her to make a prolonged attack. After throwing several blows, the person will not only be more tired, but also more vulnerable to a close counterattack. Once in close range, press your strength advantage with a strong set of punches. At this range, your opponent's advantage of longer reach will be neutralized. Avoid your opponent's attacks with dodges and body movement. When close, try to hit sensitive spots repeatedly or perform a takedown.

## Attacker of Same Height but More Power

When fighting a more powerful aggressor, keep moving and don't let your opponent prepare a powerful punch. At first, keep the aggressor at bay with lead techniques like the jab or front kick. Keep moving and stay out of range until you see an opening or you decide on a specific strategy. Attacks to the sides of your opponent's body are usually a good idea.

Watch how the aggressor fights, and figure out when he or she is winding up to punch. Then attack with your own punch first, and move out immediately. Never attempt to slug it out with somebody who is more powerful. Never let the opponent back you into a corner where he or she can rain blows on you or wrestle you to the ground. If this type of opponent

When you are the stronger, try to stay in close to neutralize the advantage of your opponent's reach. If you are a good grappler, it is a good idea to try to cut off the opponent's defensive space by backing the person into a corner so he or she cannot outmaneuver you. Eventually you will be able to grab and perform a takedown. Grappling may be the ideal technique to finish the confrontation. Once inside your opponent's guard, make sure that you tie up the person's arms by grabbing them before attempting any throw. If the person is not easily grabbed, then step in close and launch planned barrages of punches until the opponent weakens. Mix your attacks by moving in straight on and from the side, and even charging forward when the opponent seems off balance. Appear unpredictable and

gets too close, push the person away or take any other appropriate action to put distance between you. Your aim is to wear the powerful slugger out by hitting him or her with several quick series of blows that land before the opponent can launch his or her own attack.

## Shorter and More Powerful Attacker

Try to take advantage of your longer reach. Often, shorter aggressors depend heavily on powerful hook punches. Move around your opponent so that each time the person throws a hook punch he or she is off balance. While the opponent is off balance, hit him or her with a quick series of blows, then back out of range of a counterattack. Be careful not to let the opponent in close where a punch to your body or grappling will take advantage of his or her superior strength.

Do not rush to win the fight, because this might give your opponent a chance to slip your attack and counter. A shorter, stronger opponent often provokes a charge to get in close. Plan and time your attacks very carefully so that there is little chance of being backed into close quarters with the adversary. Keep moving and vary your tempo so that the opponent can be caught off guard by an occasional sudden attack.

When going after an opponent, perform a short set of up to three blows and then move away. Some especially strong opponents can take several blows while moving in close to throw short punches or grab you. If your opponent charges, try sidestepping and circling. Hit the person at an angle if possible and then move out of range. If the adversary succeeds in getting close, try pushing the person away by placing the palm of your forward arm on his or her forehead.

Once the opponent is close enough to grab you, try a volley of quick upper-cuts along with a surprise knee kick.

Sometimes you may need to tie up the aggressor's arms in a clinch to keep from being hurt. A clinch can be done by grabbing the opponent's shoulders and then bringing your hands down onto his or her biceps, keeping your arms inside the opponent's. Once you have the opponent in a clinch, you can take advantage of it: trip or throw the person if he or she is off balance, or use a knee kick or a series of short punches. Once the clinch is broken, move out quickly so the aggressor cannot resume close fighting. A mobile defense can wear down even a very strong adversary. Use mostly straight, long range blows to maximize the distance between you. Occasionally fit in a hook when you think the opponent is vulnerable. When throwing kicks, keep them fast and aim for low targets such as the attacker's knees or shins.

Try to keep a leading punch or kick between you and your opponent, but do not throw such techniques as jabs unless the opponent is clearly in range. When throwing leads make them fast, accurate, and part of a planned set of moves or combinations to weaken the opponent. Mix front and side attacks so the opponent can't figure out your strategy. Avoid wrestling with such an opponent or tying up. Should the aggressor get in close, try to keep distance by a push if necessary. If the opponent charges, side-step and counterattack.

## Attacker of Same Height and Power

Don't underestimate someone just because that person is the same height and power as you. Take advantage of any opening by moving in with a quick series of punches. If you don't see an opening, fake a jab to test your opponent's reaction. Once you have figured out the aggressor's strengths, try a set of fast attacks. Perform a mix of front, side, and charging attacks,

and vary your combinations to keep the attacker confused. Keep your opponent away with such techniques as jabs or front kicks. If the adversary is tired or slowing down, turn on the pressure with a series of hard, fast attacks at different levels.

Try to force such opponents to fight in the opposite style to what they seem to prefer. If they seem to want to wrestle, make them box; if they want to box, and you are a confident wrestler, grappling might be a good idea. Make sure you have a specific move in mind, however, before attempting to grapple.

## Shorter and Weaker Attacker

Size and strength alone do not determine the outcome of a fight. A smart, well-trained fighter who is shorter and weaker than his or her opponent can still win. When you are up against such a person, do not over-exert yourself by trying to finish your aggressor off too fast. The opponent's goal may be to wear you out and then finish you off when you are weakened. At first, move with slow, calm determination. Get a feel for your opponent's strengths. Let the aggressor underestimate your potential for speedy attacks so you can surprise him or her later.

Try to take advantage of your reach by fighting at long range most of the time. Once you have sized up the opponent, keep him or her on the defense by moving straight in with a strong set of well-timed combinations. Steady forward pressure should be combined with occasional charges.

Try to move your opponent into a corner so he or she can't escape. If the fighter tries to circle you, cut the person off by a lateral movement. Watch for your opponent to try to sidestep your advances. When the person uses such evasions, fake him or her into a dodge and then hit by surprise. Some smaller opponents take advantage of their mobility by cleverly staying out of range except when attacking. To draw such an opponent out, move forward and then move back. The opponent should come toward you. Once an opponent begins to move forward, catch the person off guard with a quick forward attack.

If your opponent gets too close, you can use a strong set of hand combinations or push the person away. However, if you are comfortable with grappling, take advantage of the opponent's closeness by performing a takedown. This is best done when the opponent is close and off balance or when you are in a clinch and one of you has grabbed the other's arms to tie them up. Do not try to rest in a clinch, but instead use it as a time to end the fight by wrestling the opponent into submission or catching the person off guard with a knee kick or similar technique.

---

## HANDLING TYPES OF AGGRESSORS

Opponents do not always fight the way you would expect them to based on their body type. You must adjust for an aggressor whose attack differs from what you expected. The following list describes strategies for handling aggressors with specific fighting styles.

### Quick-Win Artist

This is the type of fighter who relies on immediate action to overpower his or her opponents. A quick-win artist will often be overly anxious to end the fight. This type of opponent is generally unskilled in fighting and will rely on closing in immediately and pounding on you or taking you down.

When a quick-win artist rushes in, simply evade him or her. Immediately

after dodging, deliver a hard series of counterblows. Another alternative is to step forward quickly as the attacker rushes in and shoot a left jab to the chin, followed with a powerful right straight punch. Then withdraw to safety range and circle. This type of opponent, because of a lack of skill, will often rely upon wild, swinging punches or hooks. Do not let this intimidate you.

Your straight punches are faster than your opponent's hooks and will beat them to the mark. After a few of your punches land, the quick-win artist usually gets discouraged and gives up. This type of fighter is not used to a long fight and fears his or her inadequacies in skill and conditioning for such confrontation.

If an unskilled opponent swings both arms almost simultaneously it is called a "windmill" attack. You may defend by stepping to the side of the attack and delivering a one-two combination. Another alternative is to drop under the person's arms. Follow through with a one-two punch or any other two-punch combination that seems appropriate.

## Flashy Puncher

There are many bullies who believe thay can copy the fighting techniques in the movies and intimidate others with their superficial skills. To handle such a person, start with a strong, guarded position and keep moving. When your opponent throws a jab, move away by slipping it. Move into close range while slipping the aggressor's left jab, then deliver hard body punches and quickly withdraw.

Concentrate on your opponent's movement. You will find that, although at first the techniques may look good, there are obvious weaknesses in your opponent's balance or delivery. If you believe you are weaker than your opponent, try a kick to the knees or shins followed by a one-two combination.

If your opponent is the weaker, take advantage of your strength by moving in and grappling. Flashy punchers often fear a determined grappler.

Try to force your opponent to fight at close range, where flashy, long-range kicks or punches are useless. If your opponent does throw a fancy kick at you, just evade the kick and then move in and punch or throw the person. You could also evade the opponent's kick and follow through with your own kick to the opponent's supporting leg. Once a fancy kicker has had the supporting leg hit a few times, he or she tends to shy away from kicking. Another way to keep a flashy kicker's feet on the ground is to kick him or her in the groin immediately after evading an attack.

## Power Puncher

Some aggressors have tremendous physiques. You should not be intimidated, however, by an opponent's size. Big arms do not necessarily deliver powerful punches. Often, such muscular individuals have poor punching form and therefore little power in their blows. Even when they throw punches properly, the stiffness of their muscles may restrict their punches' power.

A heavy-slugging aggressor will generally have to get set before delivering a blow. Your best defense is to keep moving so that your opponent is not able to get set for a power punch. Move smoothly around the opponent, and each time the aggressor prepares to launch a power punch, hit first with a straight punch.

Vary the tempo of your movement. Catch your opponent by surprise by suddenly circling. You must move in to punch and then out very quickly, before your opponent can counter-attack. Never attempt to slug it out or grapple with a person whose chief weapon is a powerful physique. Distance is very important and you often will find that you should stay at a safety range unless you are launching an attack or your opponent moves within hitting distance.

When a power puncher throws a punch, evade and hit back in the interval before he or she can get ready for another attack. Try to draw out the power puncher, so that the aggressor's own punch over-extends and off-balances him or her. Then hit back at the time your opponent least expects.

## Counterattacker

You might face an opponent who relies heavily on blocking and counter-attacking. This kind of fighter can be dangerous. The aggressor's caution in sizing up your potential before launching an attack means that he or she is a thinker.

Such an opponent often makes you take the lead, and then exploits your mistakes. If you know that you are up against such an opponent, do not lead with the expected types of techniques, such as a left jab or left front kick. Instead, draw your opponent out by faking, so that he or she has to commit to some sort of action first. When your opponent acts, immediately counter with a combination of your own. Then keep the aggressor off balance by moving to the outside and striking at the person's ribs or other targets at the side of the body. Counterattackers are often dismayed when you bend your knees deeply and slip away from their attacks. If the aggressor absolutely will not take the lead, move slowly and then suddenly rush in with a fast flurry of punches and possibly foot techniques.

If your opponent appears to put heavy emphasis on blocking, then pretend to leave an opening. When the aggressor moves forward to attack this opening, dodge and move in close with a quick series of punches. Keep in mind that no matter how good the person is at blocking, no one is able to block every blow. While the opponent blocks your left arm, your right will be penetrating his or her defenses. Sooner or later, your punches will land and take their toll.

Once you have closed to grappling range, you can try a takedown if you are more powerful or a superior grappler.

## Polished Fighter

This is the most difficult type of individual to fight. However, you will find that very few bullies are polished fighters. If they were, they would not need to build their egos by picking on you.

If you believe that you are up against a skilled and polished fighter, do not let yourself be intimidated by your opponent's supposed skill. If you remain calm it will give you an emotional edge. Never allow your opponent to frighten or enrage you so that you start swinging wildly.

Once a fight has begun, commit yourself totally to the action. Do not allow your mind to wander or worry. Put your mind, body, and spirit behind everything you do.

In fighting a polished individual, you must establish the pattern of the fight. Do this by setting the opponent up with fakes, confusing him or her with your techniques, varying the tempo of your movements, and staying out of the range of your oponent's attack. Do not get locked into a particular pattern of fighting; this would allow your opponent to gauge your strengths and weaknesses so that they could be exploited.

Even an aggressor with strong fighting skills will leave openings in his or her defense. Use the best strategy given your opponent's body type. Your goal is to do the things that you do well and exploit your opponent's weaknesses. Keep moving at first and observe the aggressor's reactions. Use techniques that break your opponent's balance and use fakes to disrupt the aggressor's smooth combination of attacks. Vary the direction, tempo, and level of your attacks. He or she will be too busy trying to figure out what you are going to do to plan a strategy.

Do not try to match the polished fighter's speed. Instead, circle the opponent to neutralize his or her advantage. Move to the side of the attacker, and hit from long range with lead techniques like the left jab or front kick.

Try to gauge what techniques your opponent relies on and how fast the techniques are delivered. Watch how your opponent distributes weight in his or her stance. Analyze all of the attacker's reactions. You will usually be able to mount a strategy that will take advantage of any weakness. Your strategy should anticipate your attacker's moves so he or she can be set up for counterattack.

This book should be a starting point for those interested in bringing together techniques of boxing and wrestling for self-defense. It does not give all of the specific techniques that can be used, but instead shows how basic movements can be performed and coordinated. It is better to know a few techniques very well and be able to combine them than to know thousands of techniques and be unable to use any effectively.

The fighting techniques in this book should be practiced individually at first and then in combinations. Make sure to put together combinations of moves performed at different ranges. For example, move in with a left jab and throw a right straight punch. Follow with a left uppercut. Finish by executing one of the throws. After you practice several series of techniques at varying distances like this, your confidence and skill will grow. If you continue your training and learn additional boxing or wrestling techniques, they too can be put together in useful patterns. Develop those methods most useful for you.

Never use self-defense techniques aggressively to take advantage of

someone else. The essence of self-defense is to only use that amount of force that is necessary, not only in practice but also in a real fight.

Some specific suggestions for practicing the techniques follow:

1. Before practicing any fighting techniques, do a set of slow calisthenics to warm your body up.

2. Start out using techniques slowly, concentrating on your form. Once your form is perfected, you can work on increasing your speed.

3. Stay as loose and limber as possible while practicing. When you are tense, you slow down and tire out more quickly.

4. Practice combinations of techniques together, so that one technique flows into the next.

5. Try to practice techniques in front of a mirror, to get an idea of what they look like. This will help you improve your form.

6. When working with a partner, always use safety equipment, such as a mouthpiece, groin cup, and any other protective gear available. Any grappling should be practiced on a thick mat designed for that purpose.

7. In practicing with a partner, don't put all your force into a punch. Practice full power techniques only on a punching bag—not on a human being.

8. Do not hit your training partner, even lightly, unless he or she agrees to contact, you are both wearing safety equipment, and your training is properly supervised. During practice, never hit sensitive spots on your partner, such as the knees, groin, ribs, or nose.

9. Avoid the flashy techiques you see in movies. Instead, practice the basics to develop a proper foundation of self-defense techniques.

10. Squeeze your fist tightly just before hitting something. This will protect your hand and wrist.

Remember, any art of self-defense is only as good as the person using it. If you have self-confidence and persistence, your chance to prevail in any fight is great.

# Index

## About the Author

Fred Neff started his training in the Asian fighting arts at the age of eight and eventually specialized in karate. In 1974, Mr. Neff received a rank of fifth degree black belt in karate. The same year he was made a master of the art of kempo at a formal ceremony. He is also proficient in judo and jujitsu. Mr. Neff's study of Oriental culture has taken him to such lands as Hong Kong, Japan, the People's Republic of China, and Singapore.

For many years, Mr. Neff has used his knowledge to help and educate others. He has taught karate at the University of Minnesota, the University of Wisconsin, Hamline University and Inver Hills College in St. Paul, Minnesota. He has also organized and supervised self-defense classes for special education programs, public schools, private institutions, and city recreation departments. Included in his teaching program have been classes for law enforcement officers.

He has received many awards for his active community involvement, including the City of St. Paul Citizen of the Month Award in 1975, a Commendation for Distinguished Service from the Sibley County Attorney's Of-

fice in 1980, the WCCO Radio Good Neighbor Award in 1985, and the Lamp of Knowledge Award from the Twin Cities Lawyers Guild in 1986.

Fred Neff graduated with high distinction from the University of Minnesota College of Education in 1970. In 1976, he received his J.D. degree from William Mitchell College of Law in St. Paul, Minnesota. Mr. Neff is now a practicing attorney in Minneapolis, Minnesota.

He is the author of fourteen books, including *Everybody's Book of Self-Defense, Karate is for Me, Lessons from the Western Warriors, Lessons from the Art of Kempo, Lessons from the Samurai,* and the eight books which make up Fred Neff's Self-Defense Library.